Sacred Solos

Level Three

Supplement to All Piano and Keyboard Methods

Compiled, Arranged, and Edited by Wesley Schaum

Foreword

This series of sacred solos includes favorite hymns, gospel songs, spirituals and sacred music from the classical repertoire. The selections have been made to appeal to students of all ages and also with regard to popularity in many different churches. Some of the hymn tunes may be known with different titles and lyrics.

Selections with two verses are arranged so that the *second verse* is in a *different key*. *An **asterisk** indicates that the second verse is a *transposed* version of the first verse. Transposing is valuable for ear training.

Contents

To access audio visit:
www.halleonard.com/mylibrary

7249-4313-2047-7237

ISBN 978-1-4950-8217-7

EXCLUSIVELY DISTRIBUTED BY

7777 W. BLUEMOUND RD. P.O. BOX 13819 MILWAUKEE, WI 53213

Visit Hal Leonard Online at
www.halleonard.com

All Hail the Power of Jesus' Name

Edward Perronet

Oliver Holden

Stand Up, Stand Up for Jesus

George Duffield, Jr.

George J. Webb

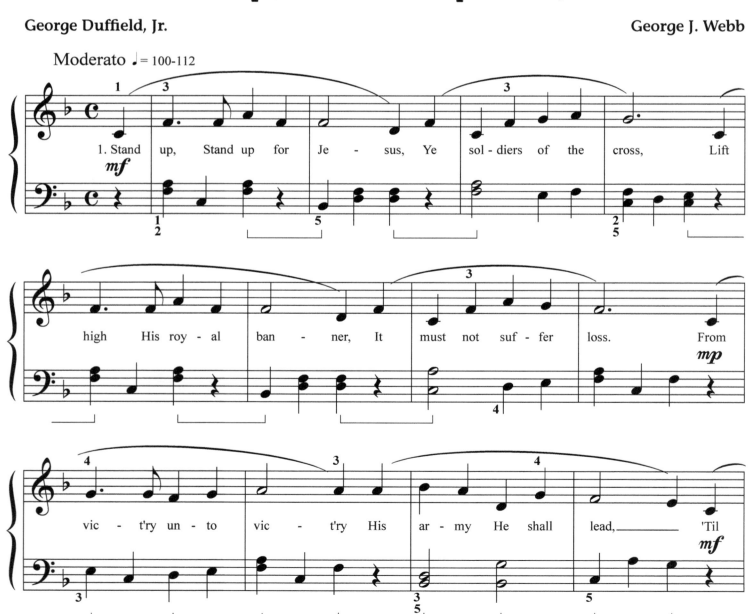

Moderato ♩ = 100-112

1. Stand up, Stand up for Je - sus, Ye sol - diers of the cross, Lift

high His roy - al ban - ner, It must not suf - fer loss. From

vic - t'ry un - to vic - t'ry His ar - my He shall lead,_____ 'Til

Blest Be the Tie That Binds

John Fawcett

Johann G. Nägeli

Come, Ye Thankful People, Come

Henry Alford

George J. Elvey

Come, ye thank-ful peo-ple, come, Raise the song of har-vest home;

All is safe-ly gath-ered in, Ere the win-ter storms be-gin.

God, our Mak-er, doth pro-vide For our wants to be sup-plied,

Come to God's own tem-ple, come, Raise the song of har-vest home.

This Is My Father's World

Maltbie D. Babcock

Franklin L. Sheppard

Dolce ♩ = 104-116

p

1. This__ is my Fa - ther's world, And__ to my lis - t'ning ears, All

na - ture sings, and__ 'round me rings The mu - sic of the__ spheres. *mf* This

is my Fa - ther's world: I__ rest me in the thought *mp* Of

Lonesome Road

African-American Spiritual

Lead On, O King Eternal

Ernest W. Shurtleff

Henry Smart

Holy, Holy, Holy

Reginald Heber

John B. Dykes

Andantino ♩ = 96-104

1. Ho - ly, Ho - ly, Ho - ly! Lord God Al - might - y!

Ear - ly in the morn - ing our song shall rise to Thee.

Ho - ly, Ho - ly, Ho - ly! Mer - ci - ful and might - y.

Fairest Lord Jesus

Anonymous   **Richard S. Willis**

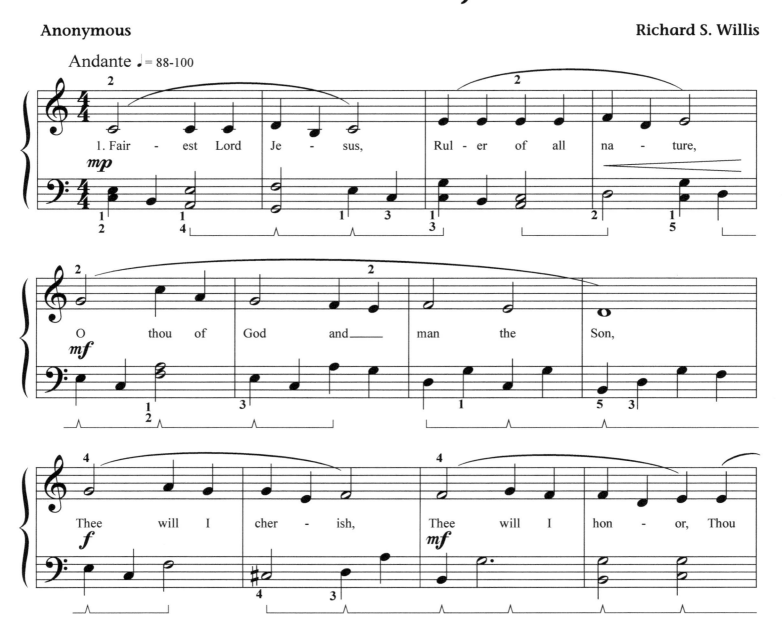

Sweet Hour of Prayer

William W. Walford

William B. Bradbury

God of Our Fathers

Daniel C. Roberts

George W. Warren

Andantino ♩ = 96-108

God of our fa - - thers, whose al - might - y hand

Leads forth in beau - - ty all the star - ry band,

Of shin - ing worlds in splen - dor through the skies,

Our grate - ful songs be - fore Thy throne a - rise.

Amazing Grace

John Newton   **Early American Melody**

1. A-maz-ing grace how sweet the sound That saved a wretch like me!

f I once was lost, but now am

My Heart Ever Faithful

J.S. Bach

Blessed Assurance

Fanny Crosby

Phoebe P. Knapp

Ave Maria

Bach-Gounod

MORE GREAT SCHAUM PUBLICATIONS

FINGERPOWER®

by John W. Schaum

Physical training and discipline are needed for both athletics and keyboard playing. Keyboard muscle conditioning is called technique. technique exercises are as important to the keyboard player as workouts and calisthenics are to the athlete. Schaum's *Fingerpower®* books are dedicated to development of individual finger strength and dexterity in both hands.

00645334	Primer Level – Book Only	$7.99
00645016	Primer Level – Book/Audio	$9.99
00645335	Level 1 – Book Only	$6.99
00645019	Level 1 – Book/Audio	$8.99
00645336	Level 2 – Book Only	$7.99
00645022	Level 2 – Book/Audio	$9.99
00645337	Level 3 – Book Only	$6.99
00645025	Level 3 – Book/Audio	$7.99
00645338	Level 4 – Book Only	$6.99
00645028	Level 4 – Book/Audio	$9.99
00645339	Level 5 Book Only	$7.99
00645340	Level 6 Book Only	$7.99

FINGERPOWER® ETUDES

Melodic exercises crafted by master technique composers. Modified or transposed etudes provide equal hand development with a planned variety of technical styles, keys, and time signatures.

00645392	Primer Level	$6.99
00645393	Level 1	$6.99
00645394	Level 2	$6.99
00645395	Level 3	$6.99
00645396	Level 4	$6.99

FINGERPOWER® FUN

arr. Wesley Schaum
Early Elementary Level

Musical experiences beyond the traditional *Fingerpower®* books that include fun-to-play pieces with finger exercises and duet accompaniments. Short technique preparatory drills (finger workouts) focus on melodic patterns found in each piece.

00645126	Primer Level	$6.95
00645127	Level 1	$6.99
00645128	Level 2	$6.95
00645129	Level 3	$6.99
00645144	Level 4	$6.95

FINGERPOWER® POP

arr. by James Poteat

10 great pop piano solo arrangements with fun technical warm-ups that complement the *Fingerpower®* series! Can also be used as motivating supplements to any method and in any learning situation.

00237508	Primer Level	$9.99
00237510	Level 1	$9.99
00282865	Level 2	$9.99
00282866	Level 3	$9.99
00282867	Level 4	$10.99

FINGERPOWER® TRANSPOSER

by Wesley Schaum
Early Elementary Level

This book includes 21 short, 8-measure exercises using 5-finger patterns. Positions are based on C,F, and G major and no key signatures are used. Patterns involve intervals of 3rds, 4ths, and 5ths up and down and are transposed from C to F and F to C, C to G and G to C, G to F and F to G.

00645150	Primer Level	$6.95
00645151	Level 1	$6.95
00645152	Level 2	$6.95
00645154	Level 3	$6.95
00645156	Level 4	$6.99

JUMBO STAFF MANUSCRIPT BOOK

This pad features 24 pages with 4 staves per page.

00645936		$4.25

CERTIFICATE OF MUSICAL ACHIEVEMENT

Reward your students for their hard work with these official 8x10-inch certificates that you can customize. 12 per package.

00645938		$6.99

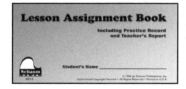

SCHAUM LESSON ASSIGNMENT BOOK

by John Schaum

With space for 32 weeks, this book will help keep students on the right track for their practice time.

00645935		$3.95

www.halleonard.com

Prices, contents, and availability subject to change without notice.